I0463963

Turtles Coloring Book For Adults

This book belongs to:

____

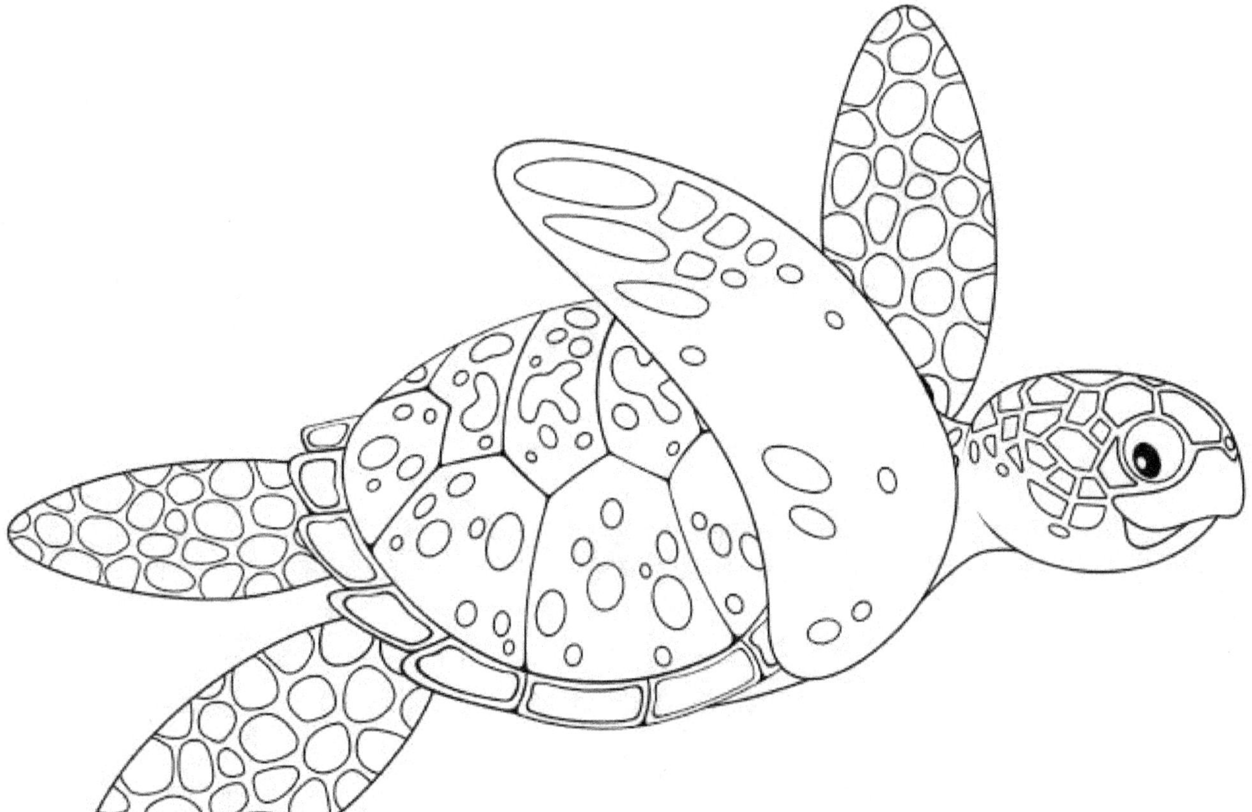

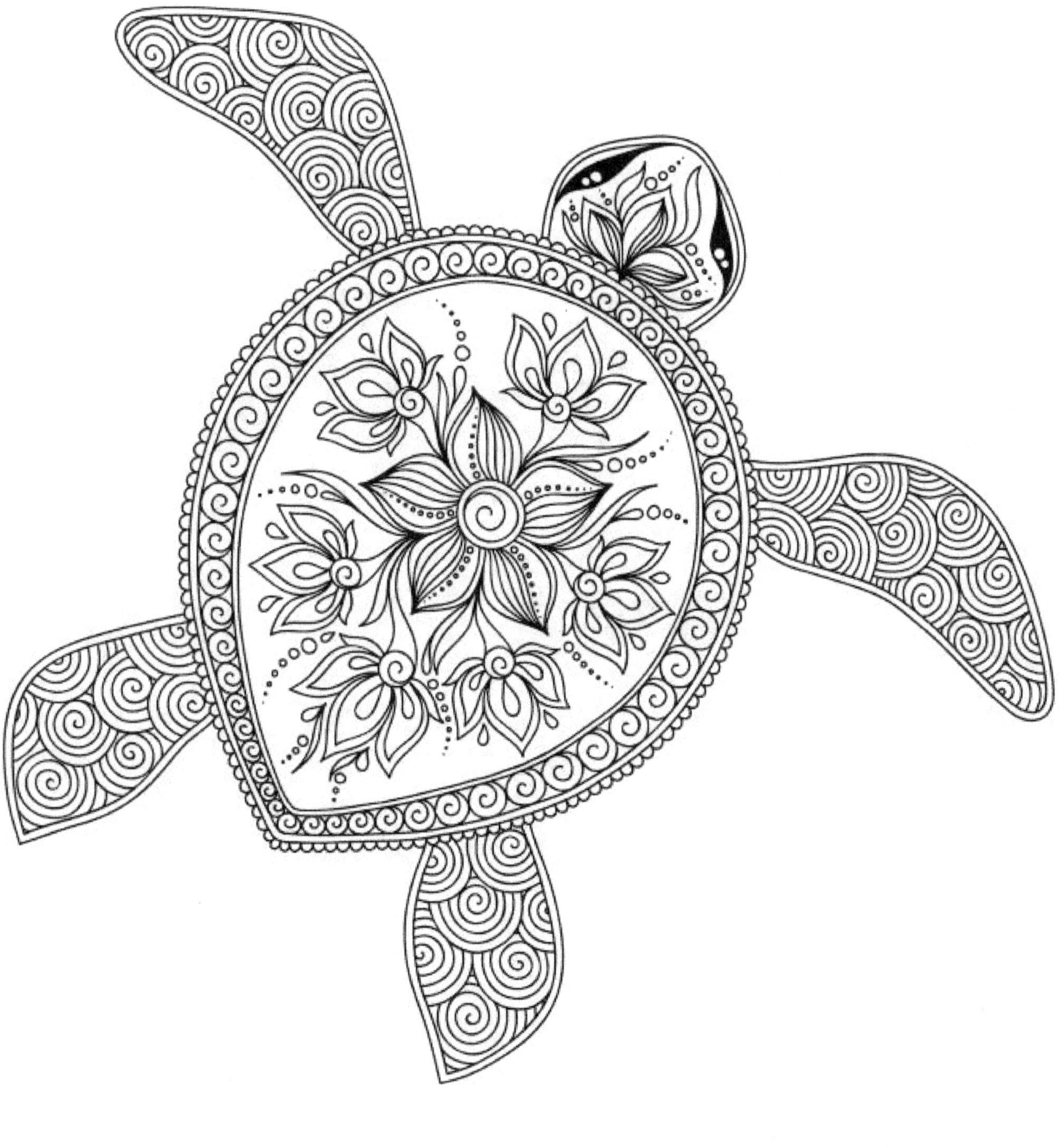

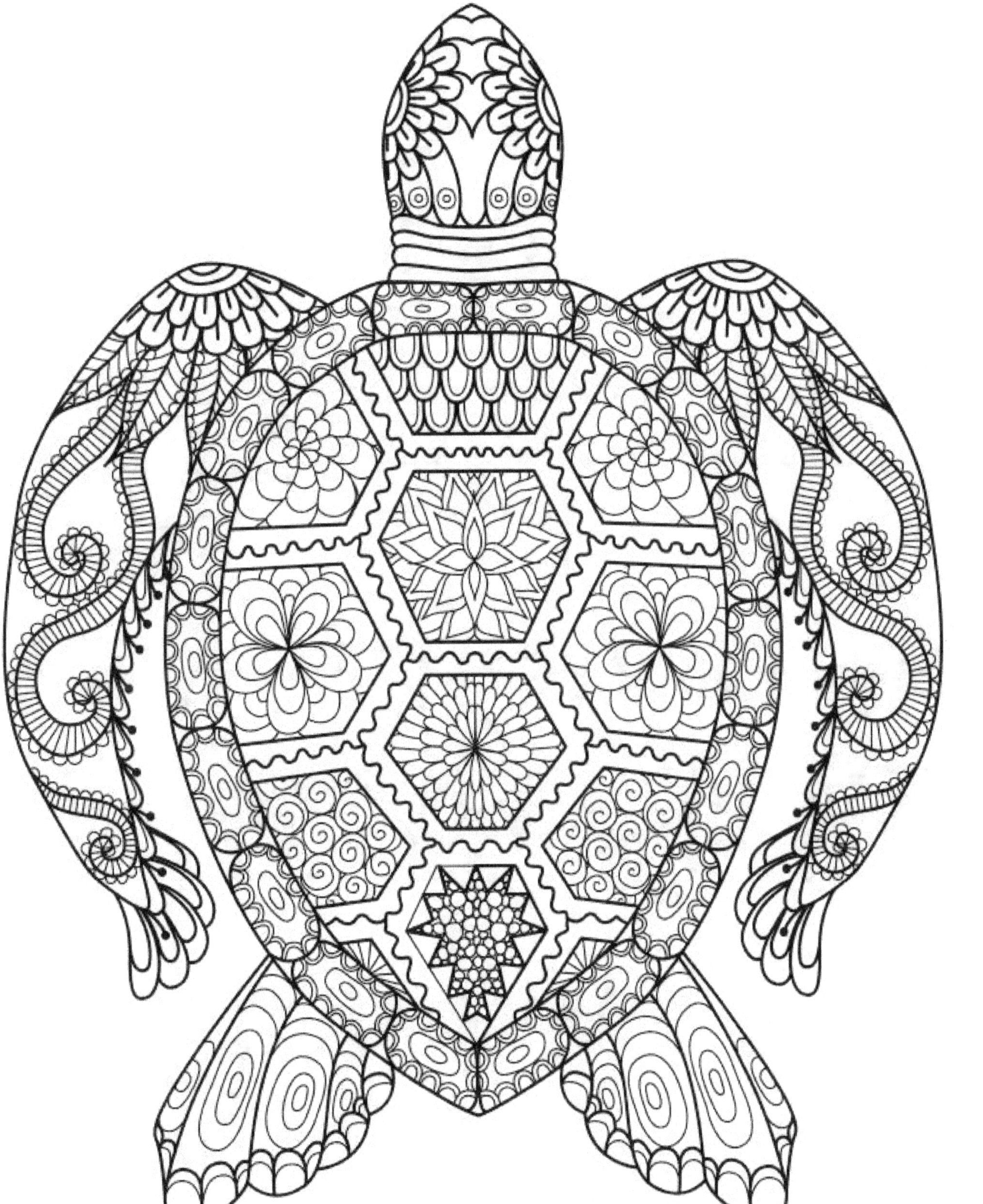

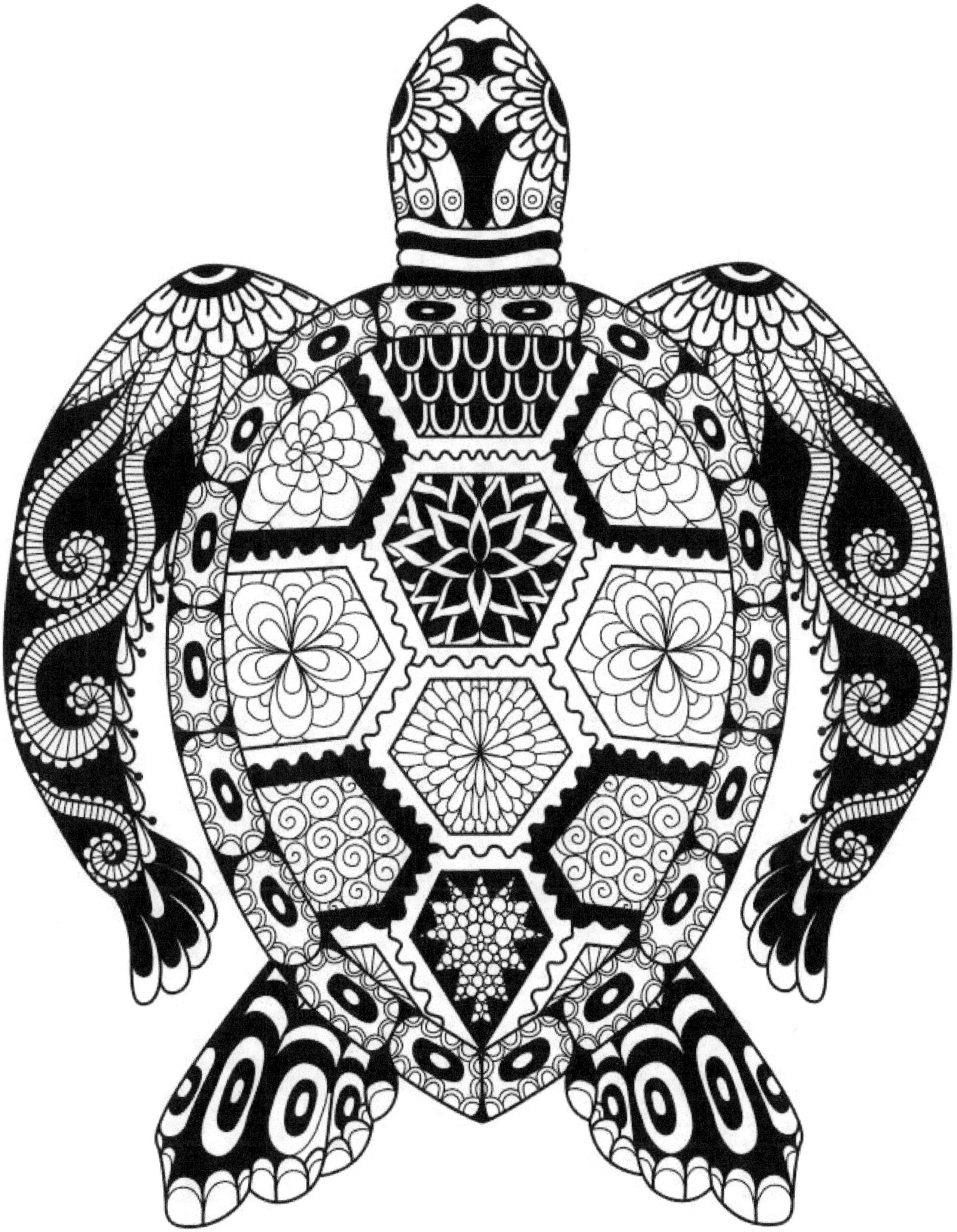

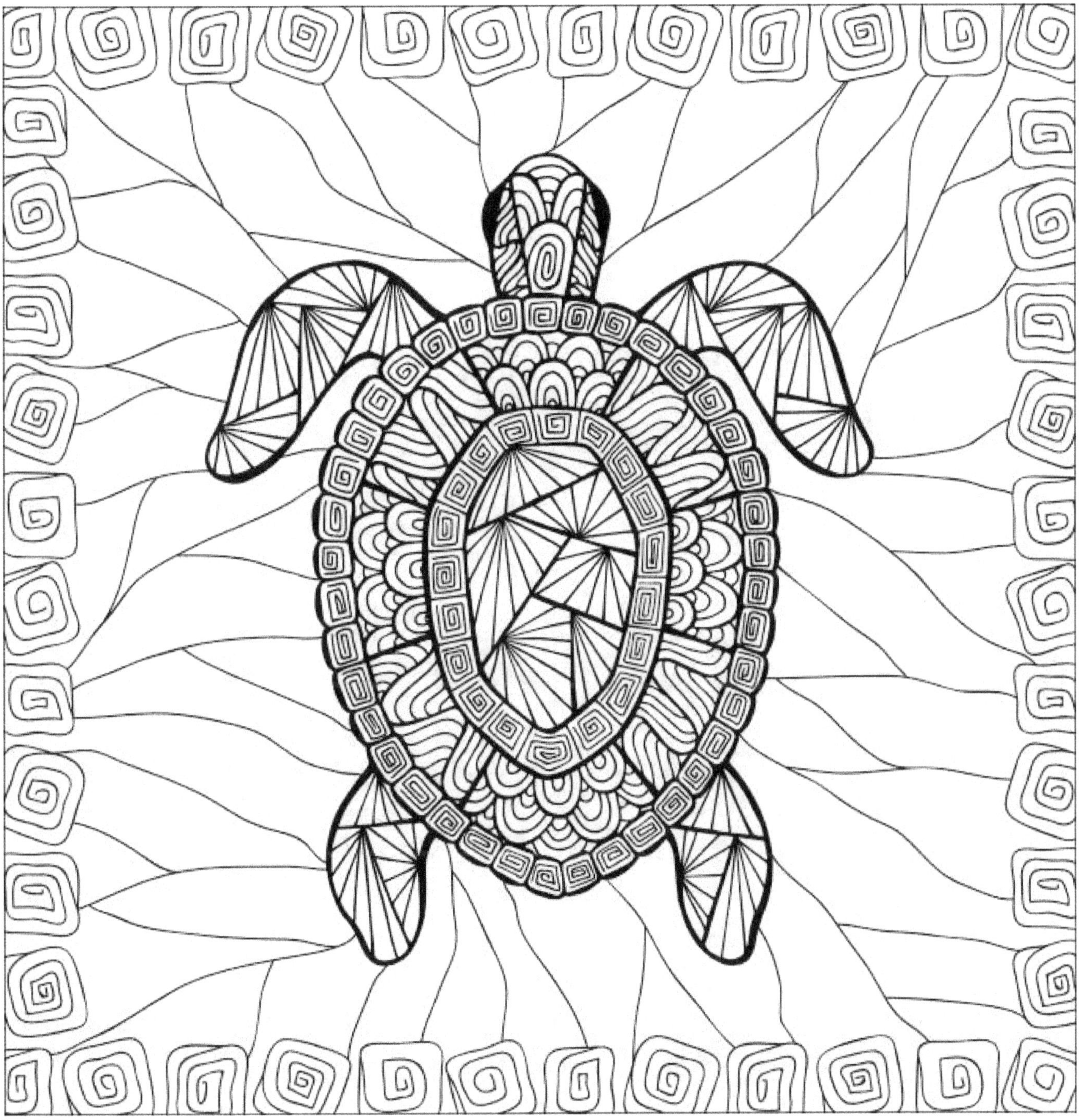

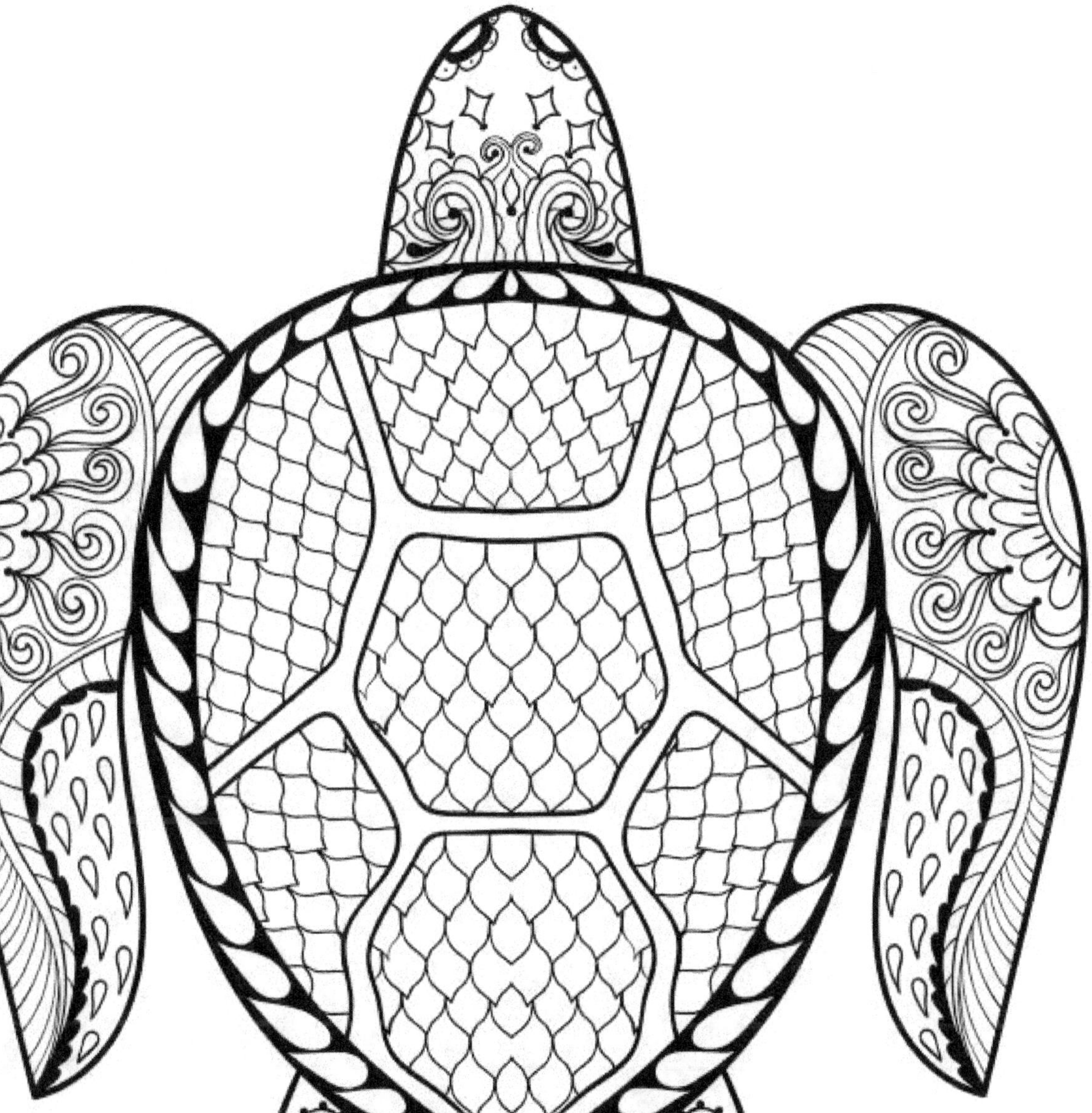

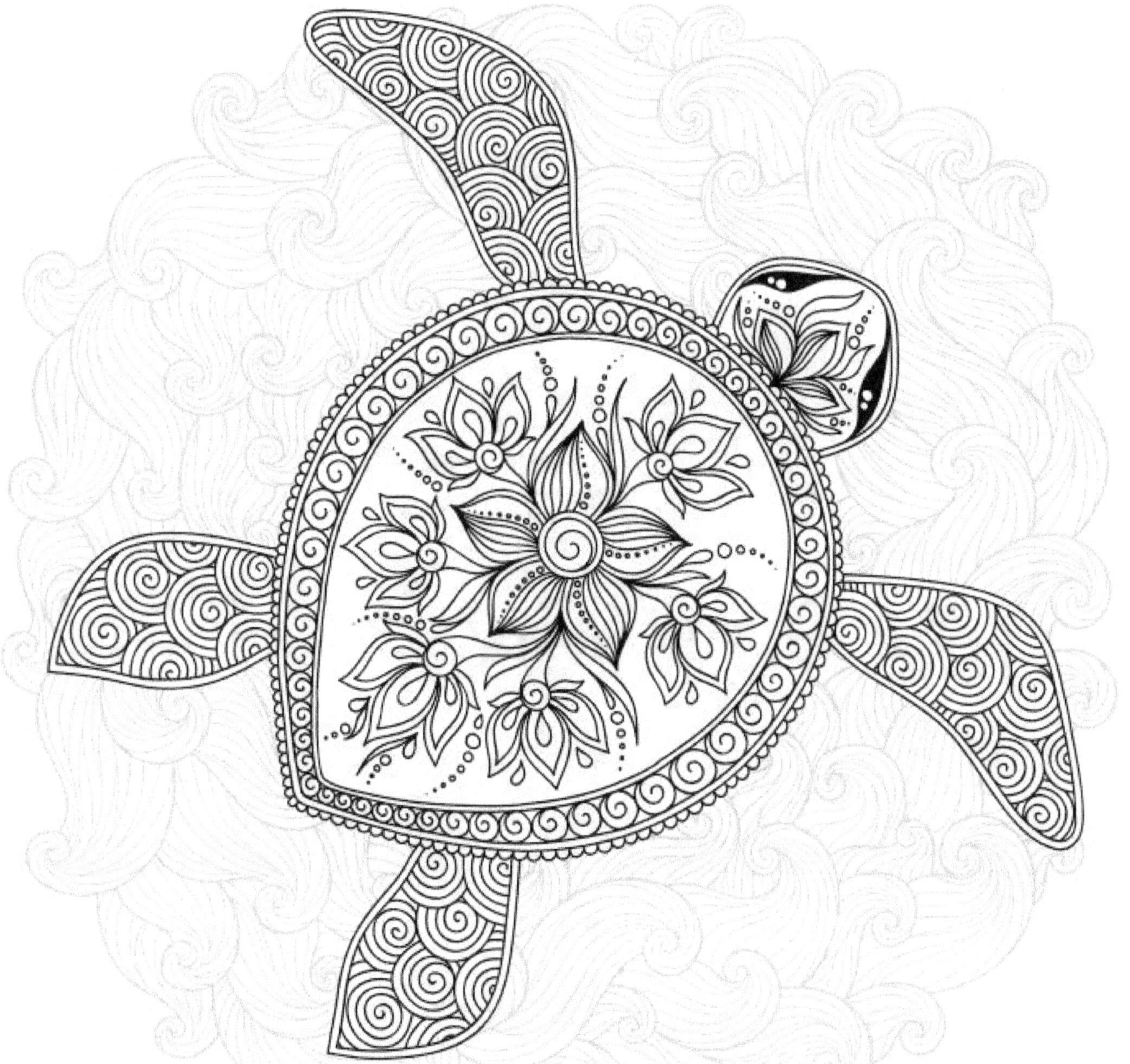

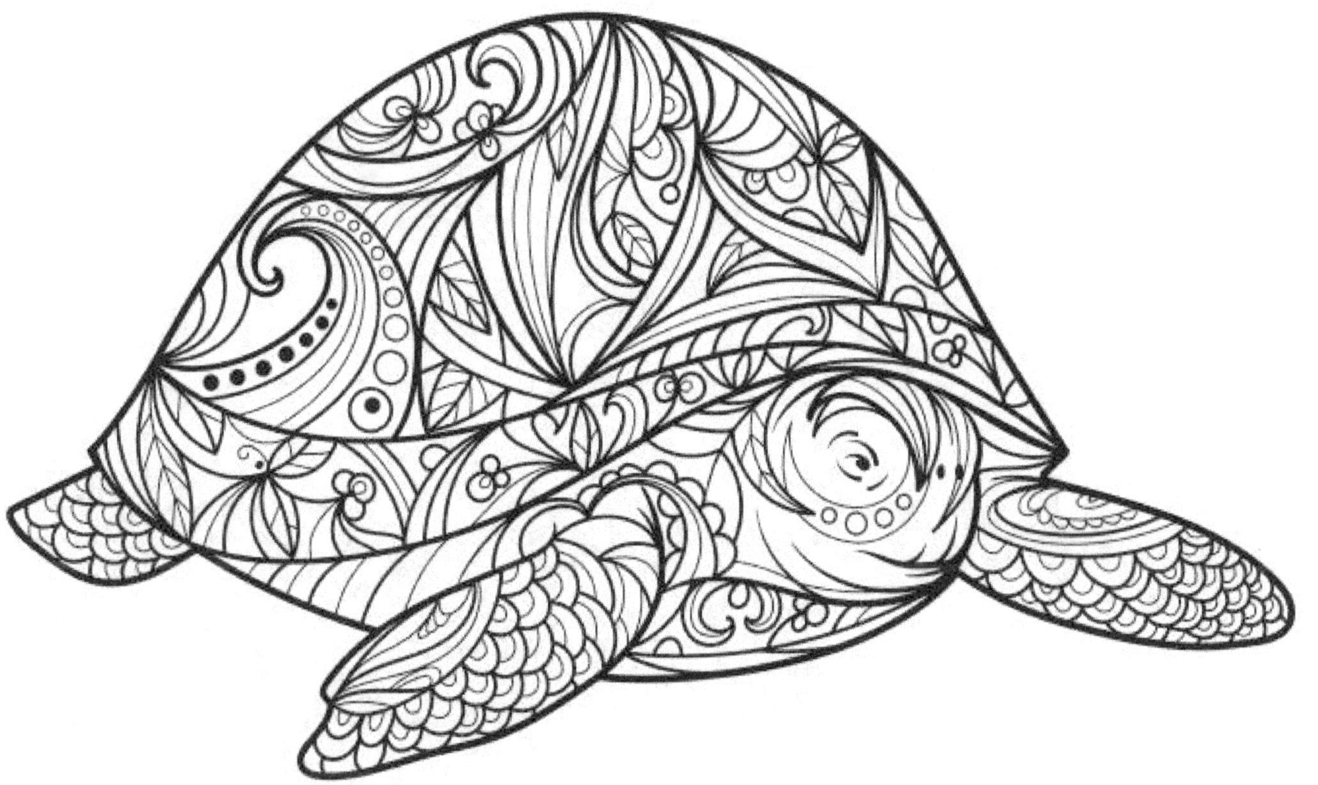

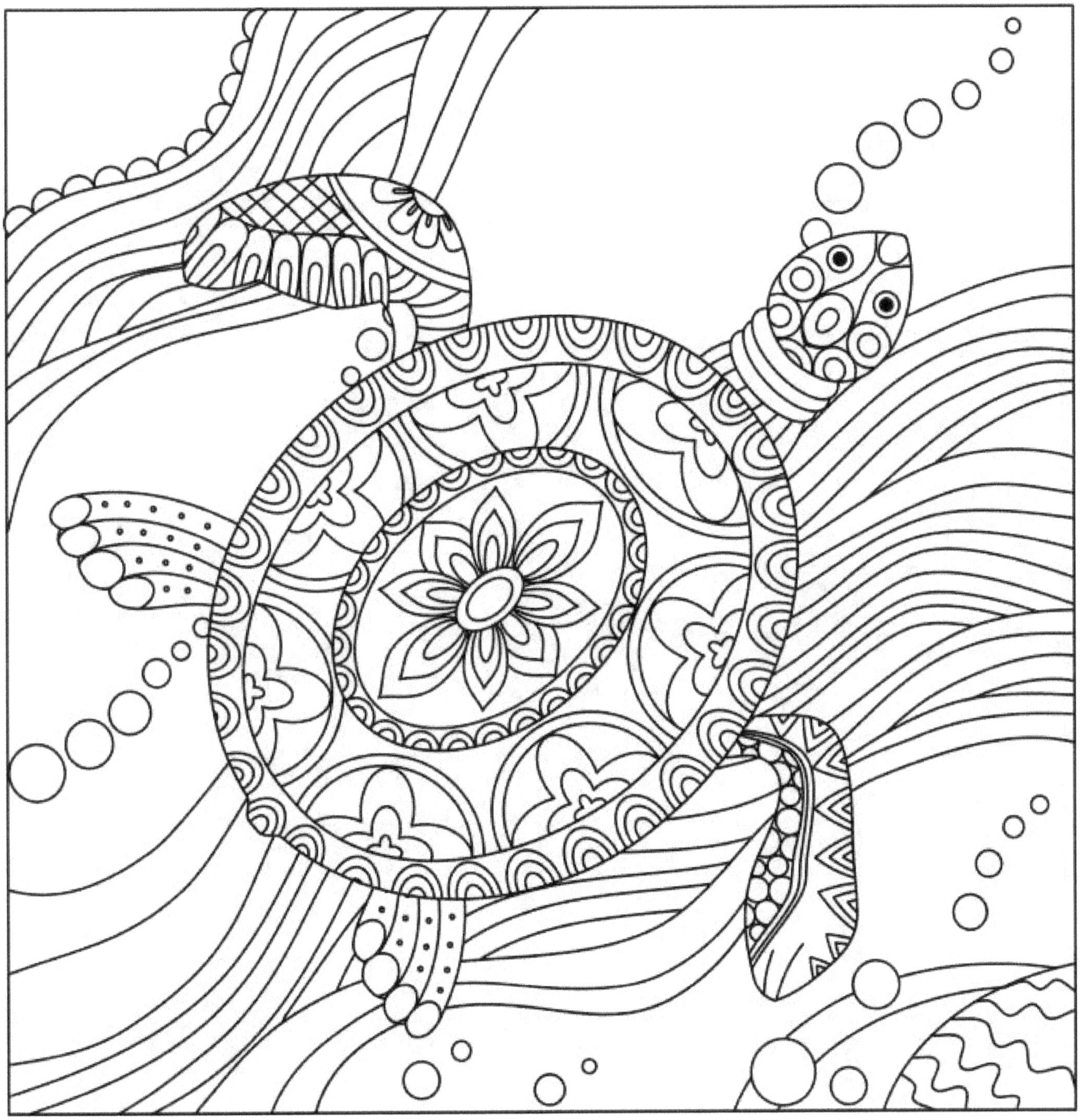

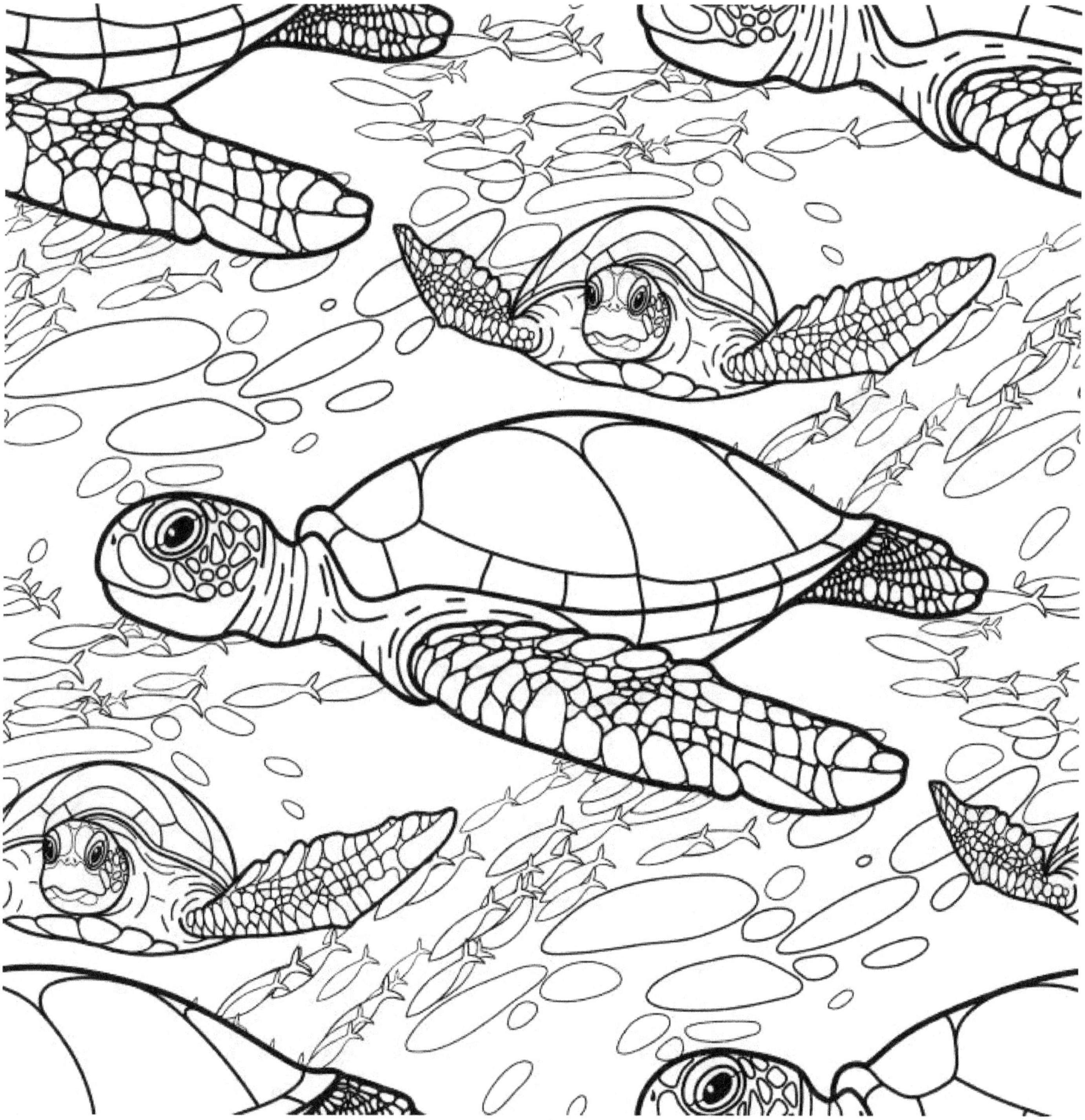

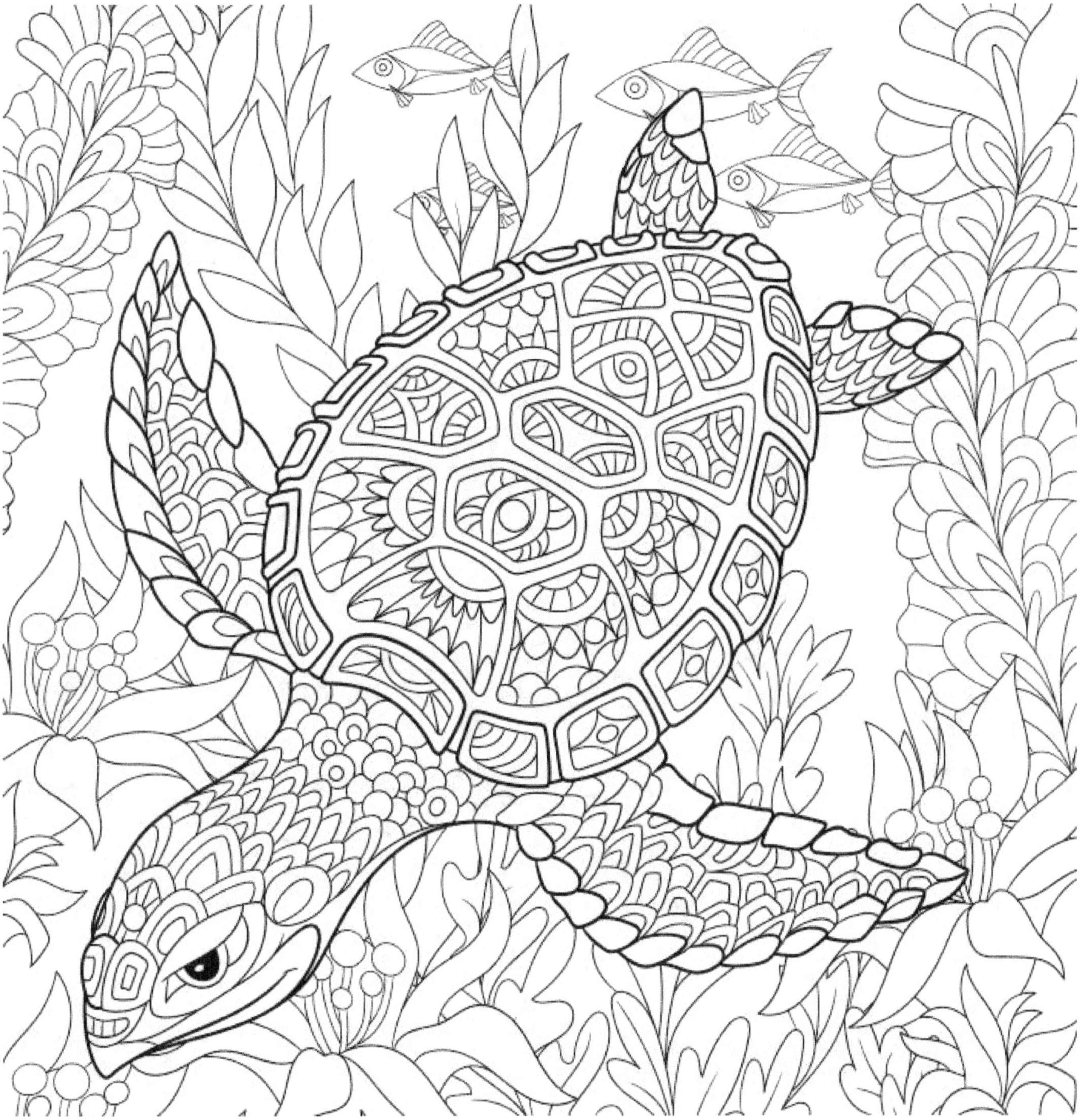

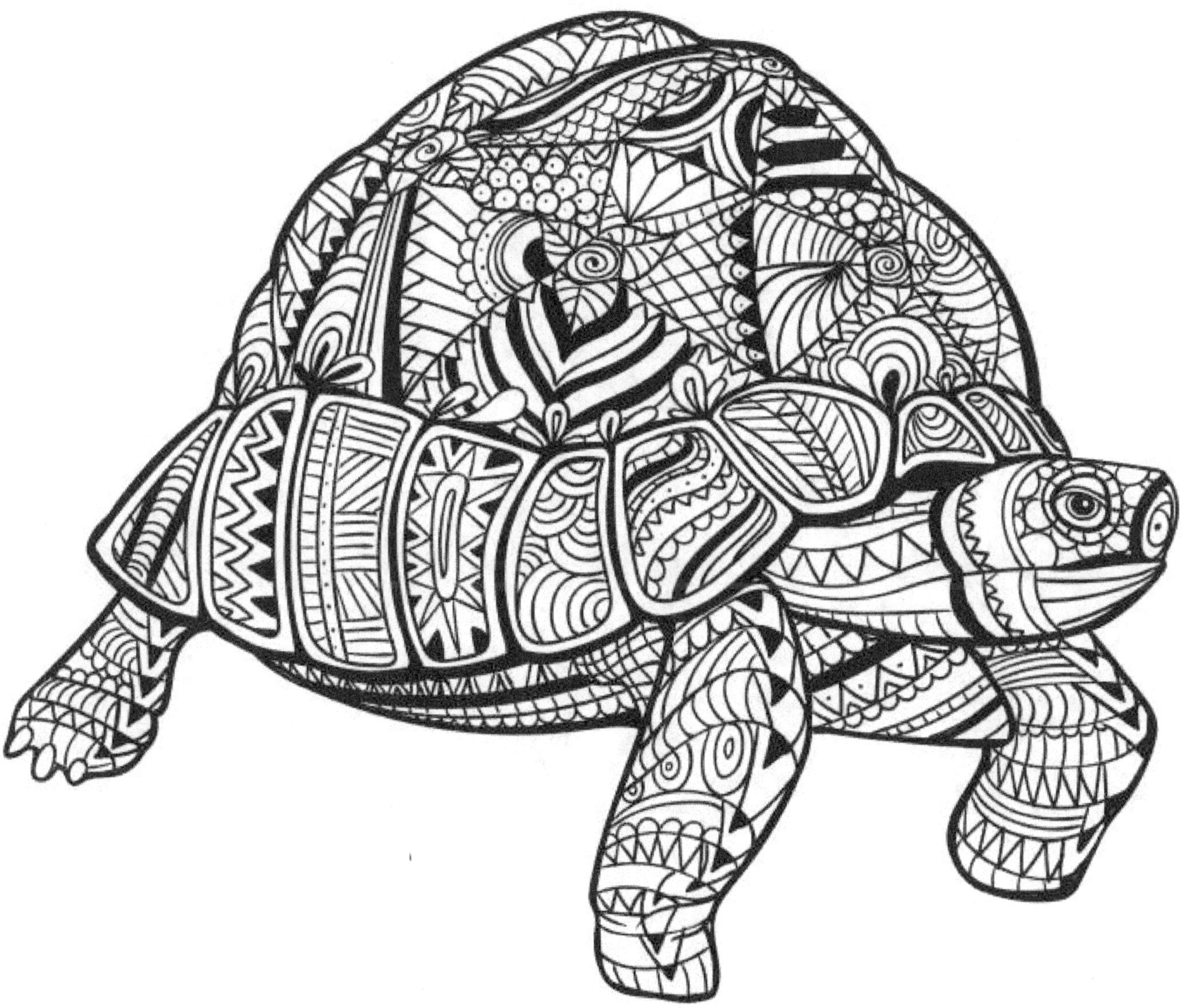

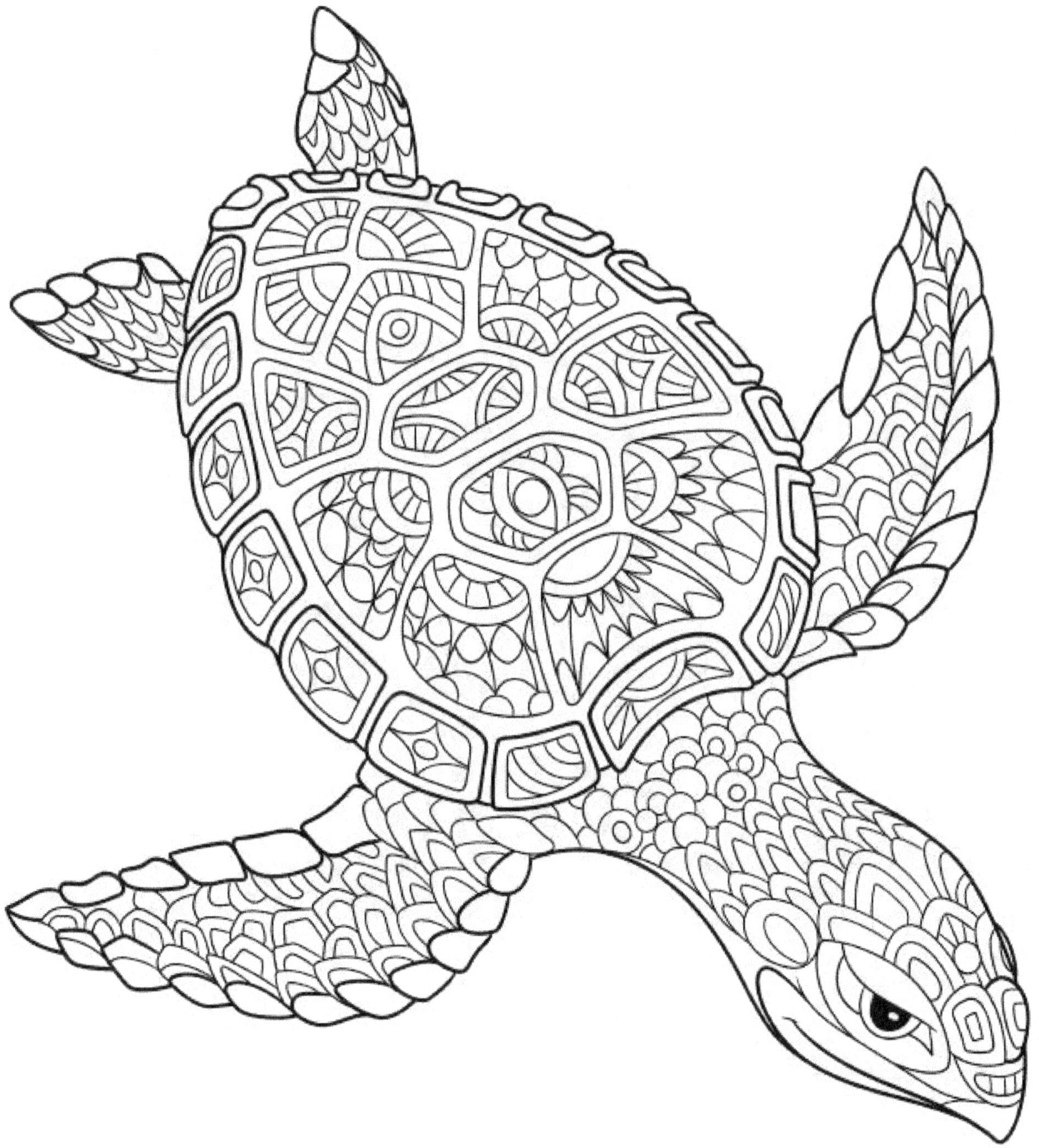

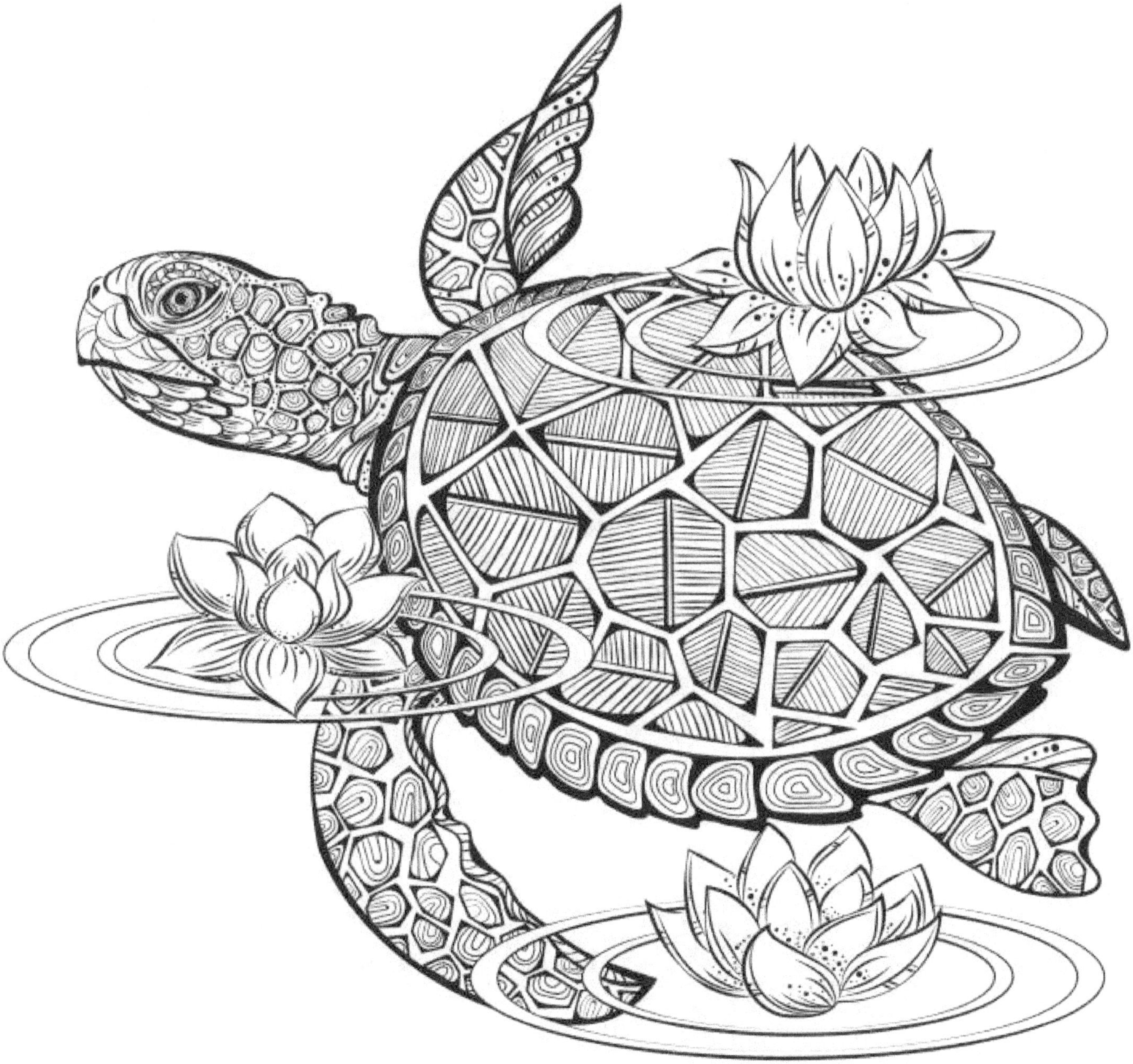

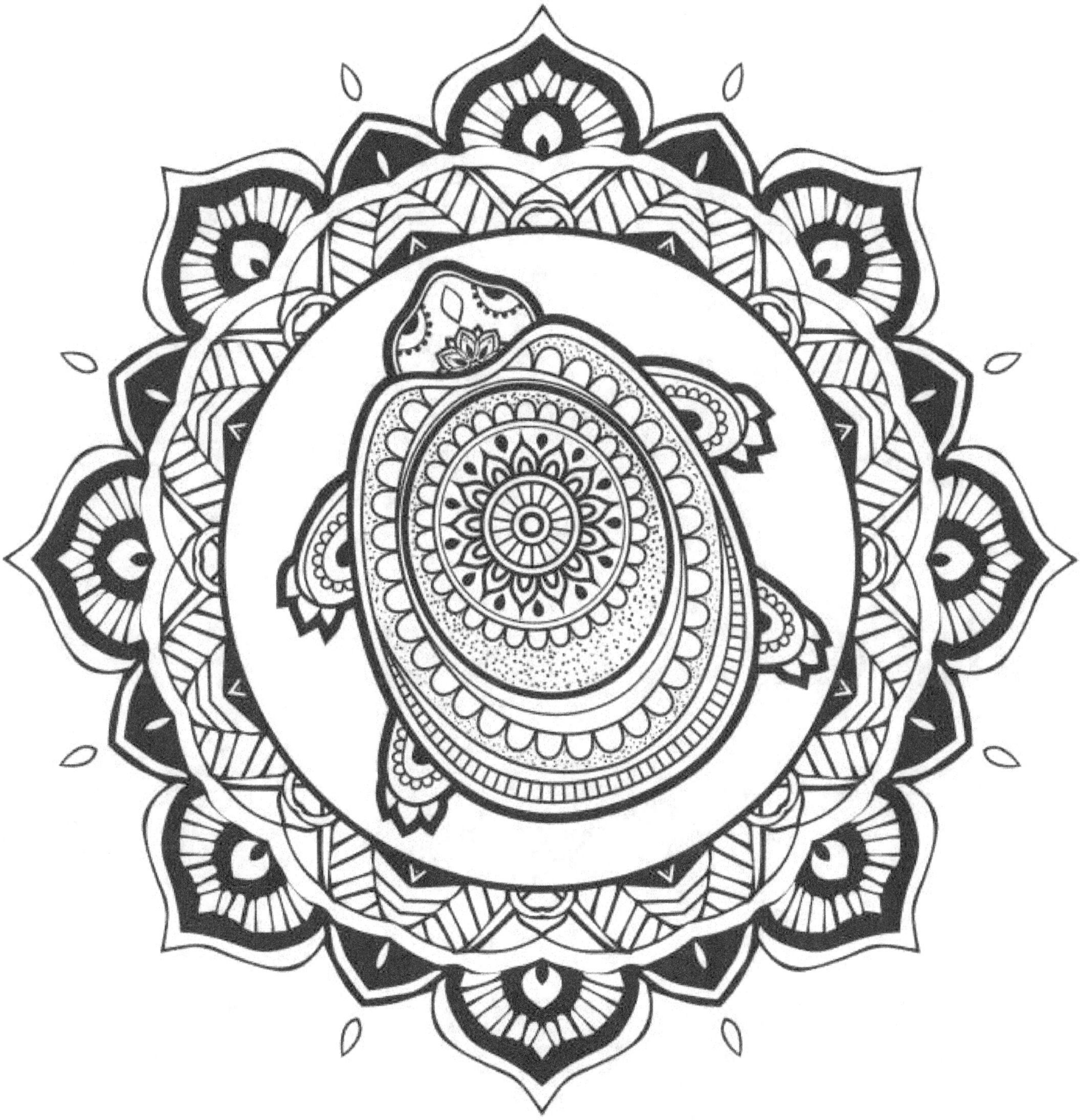

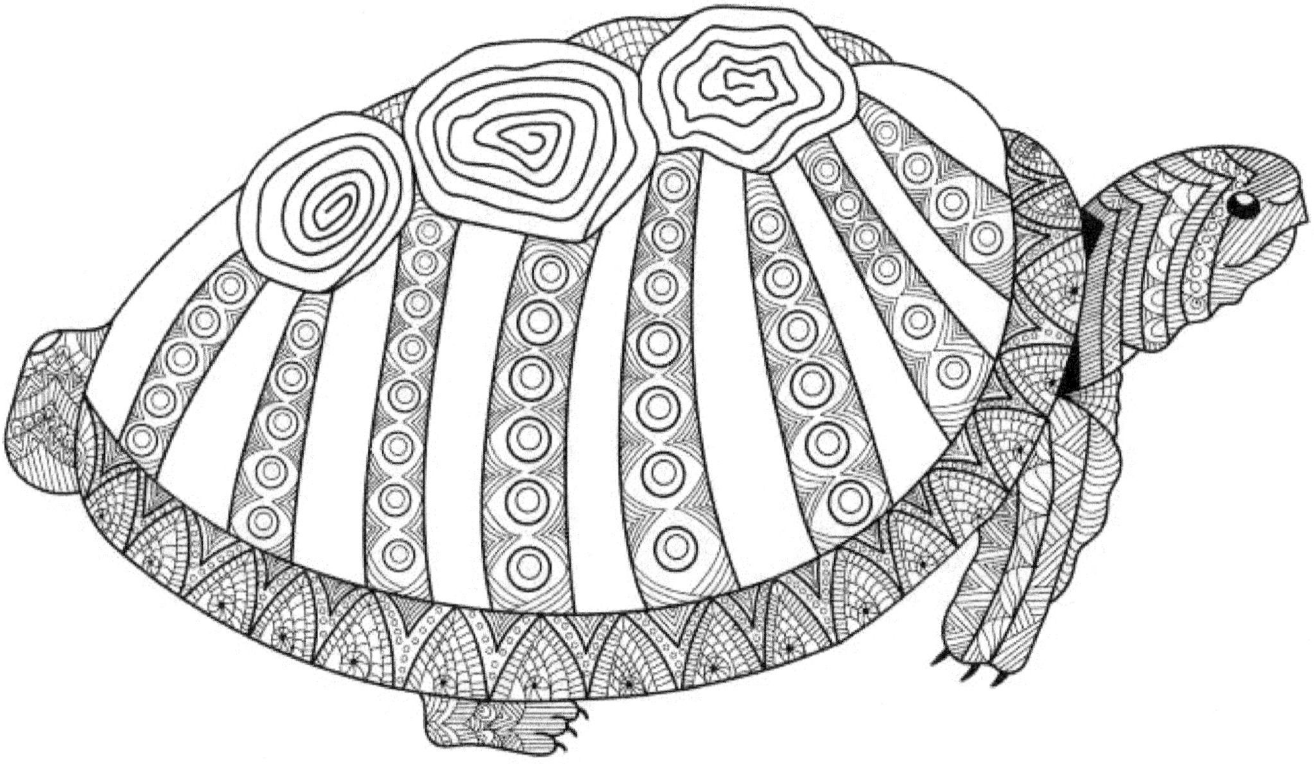

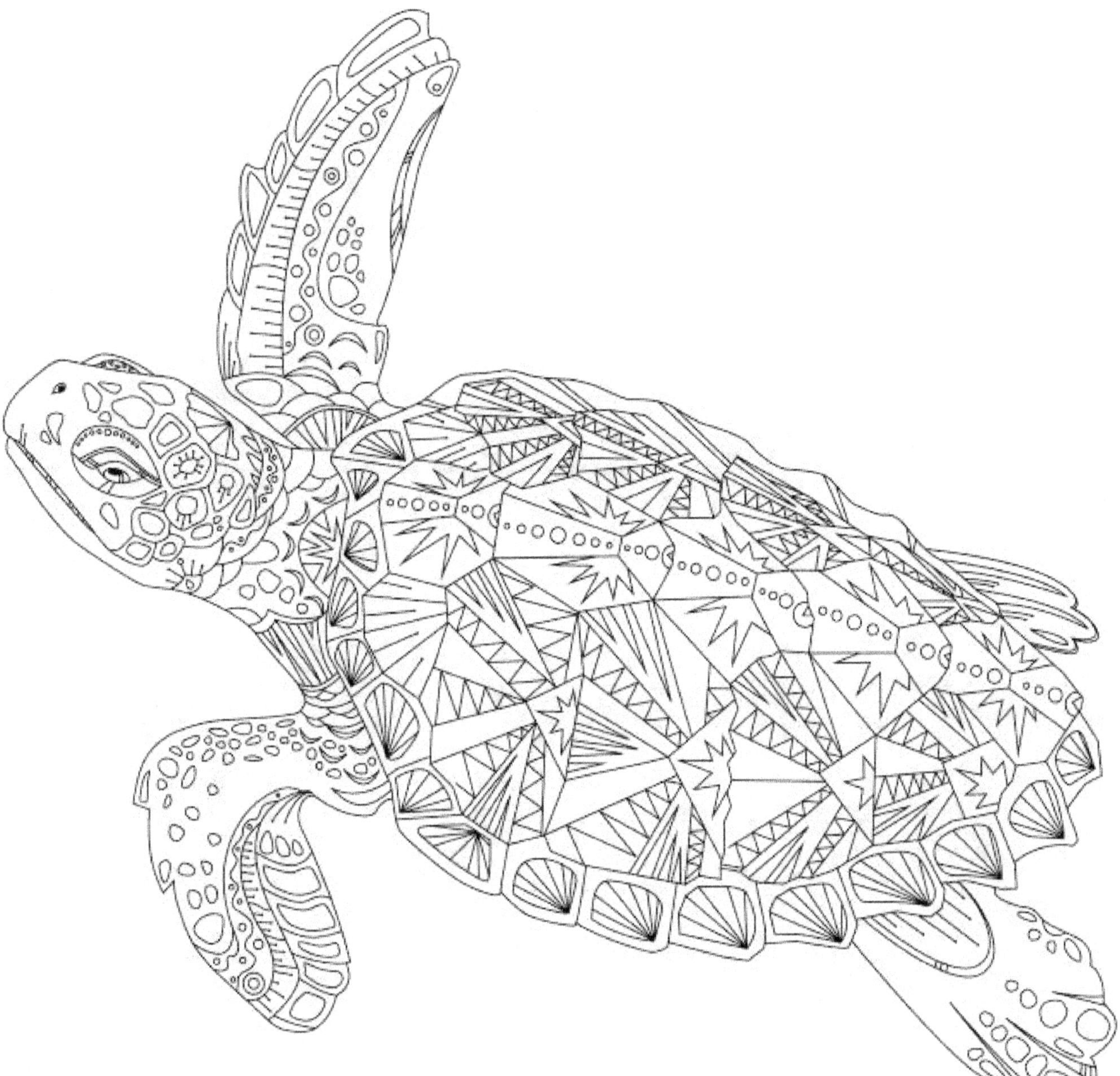

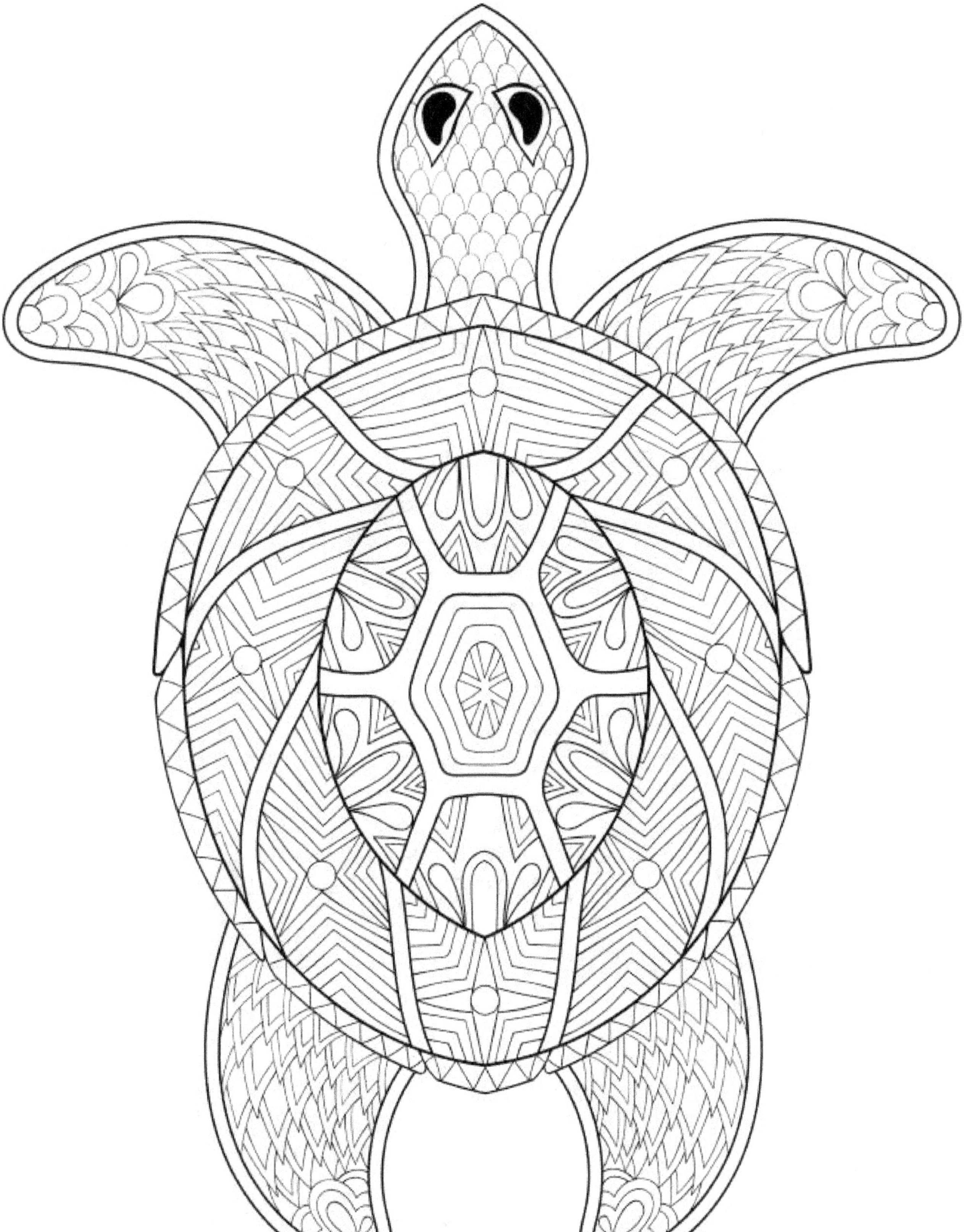

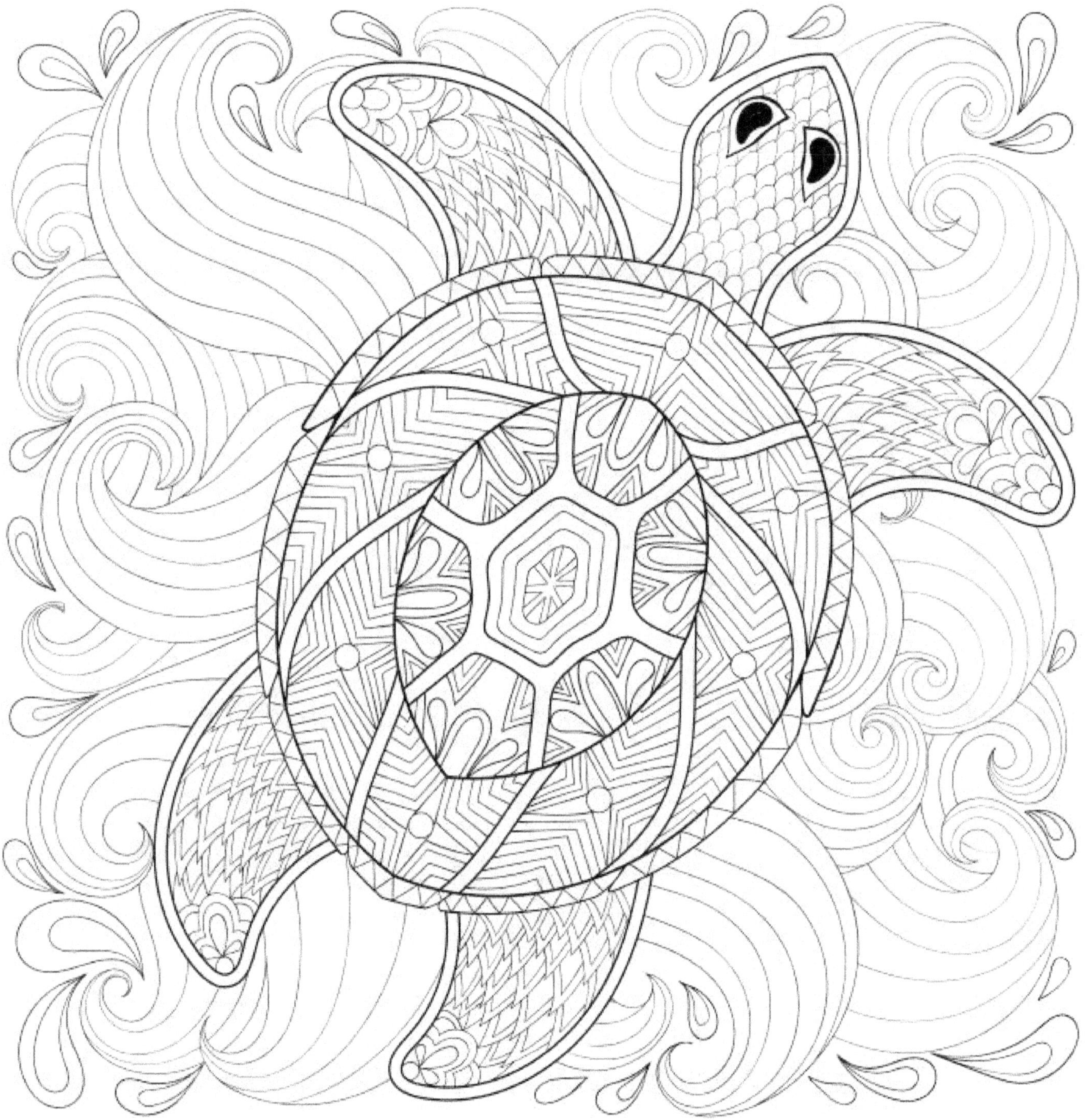

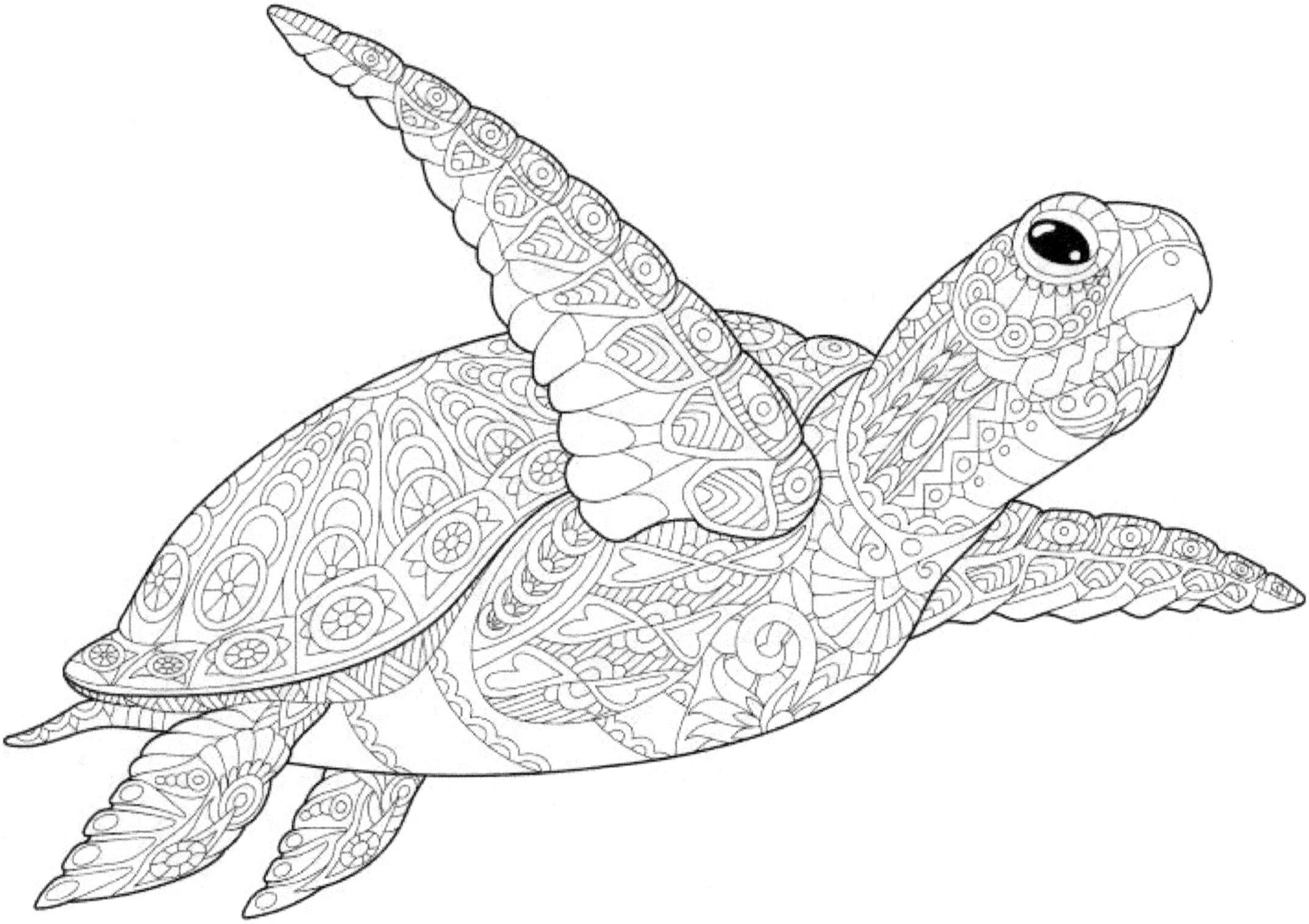

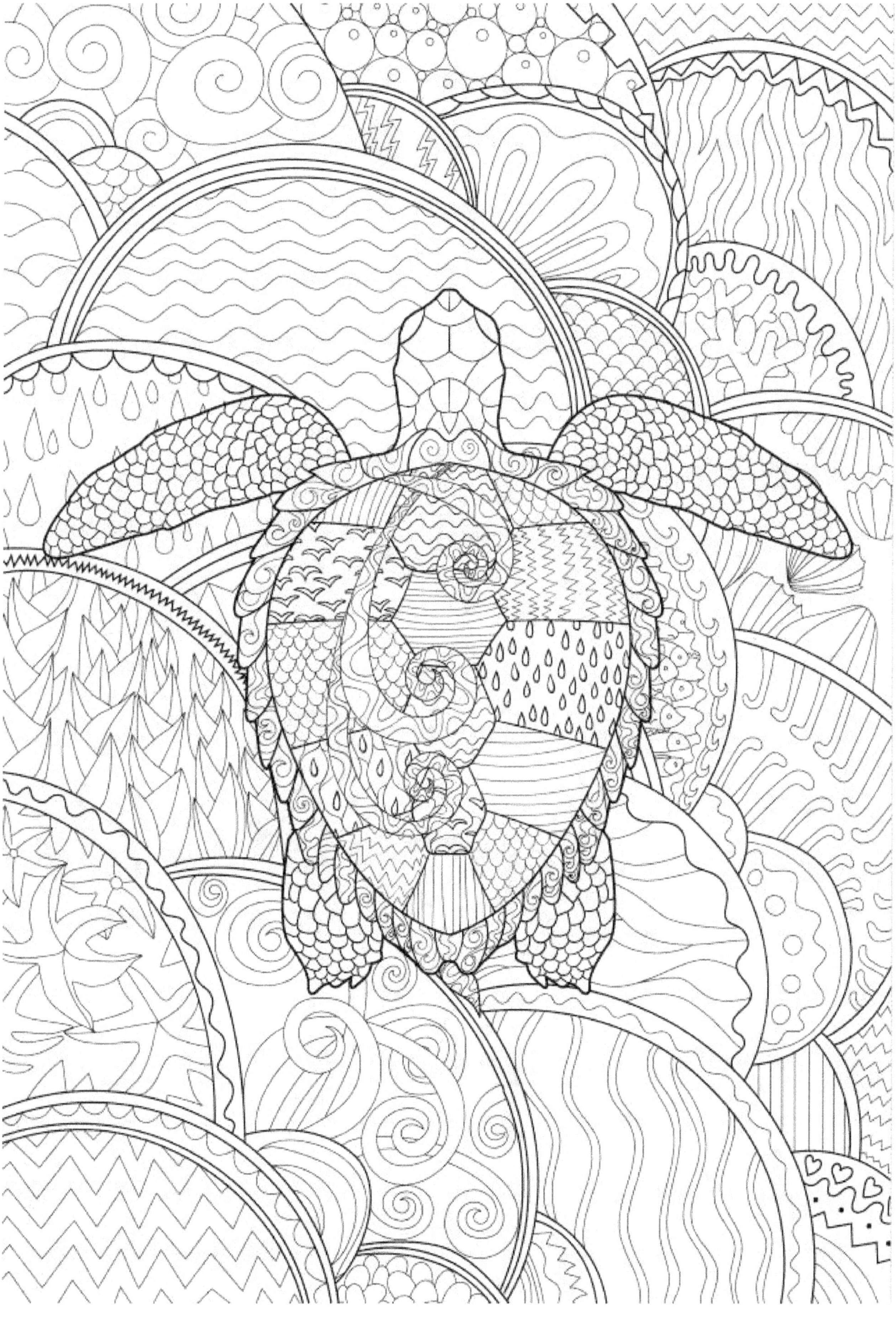

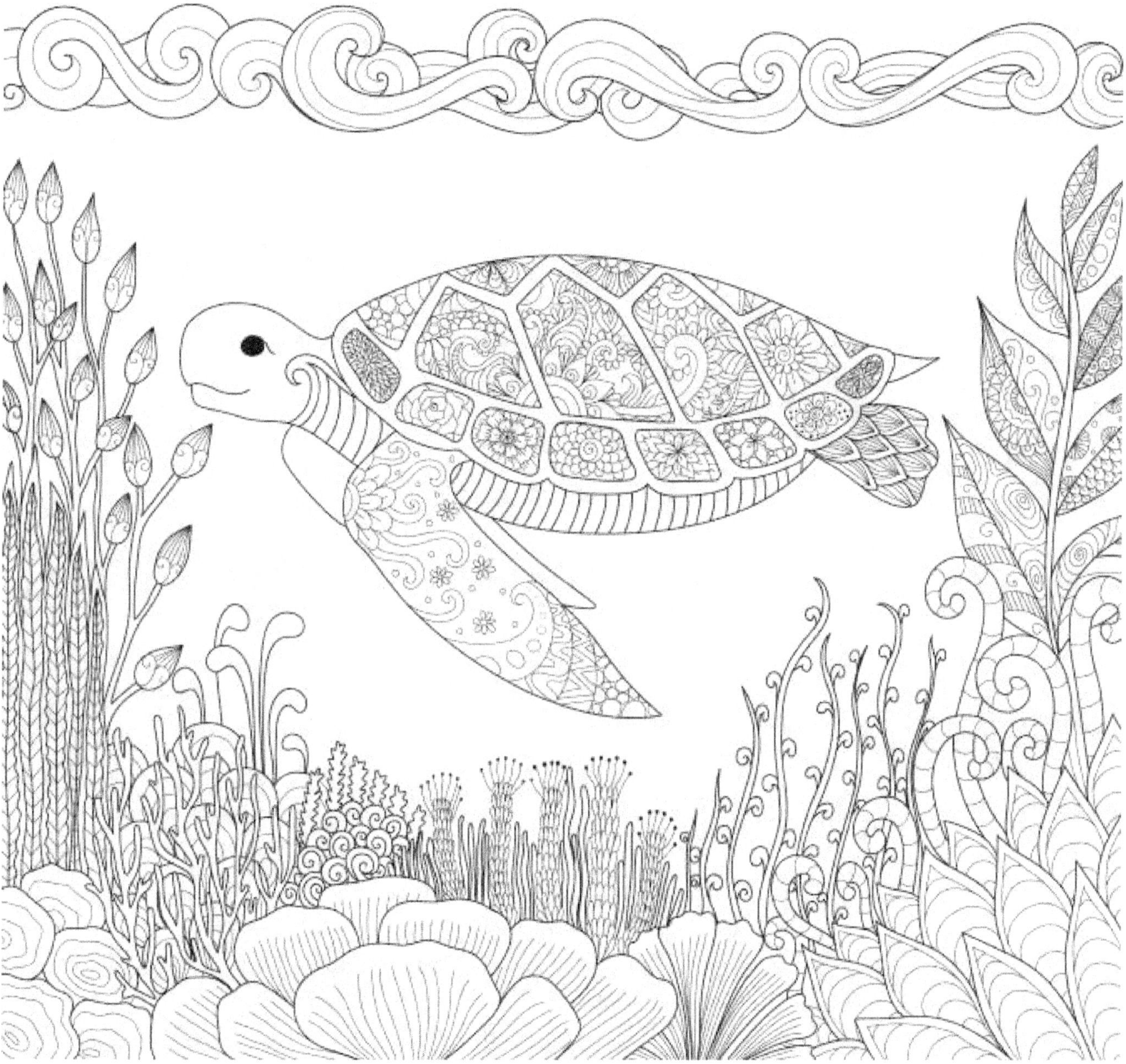

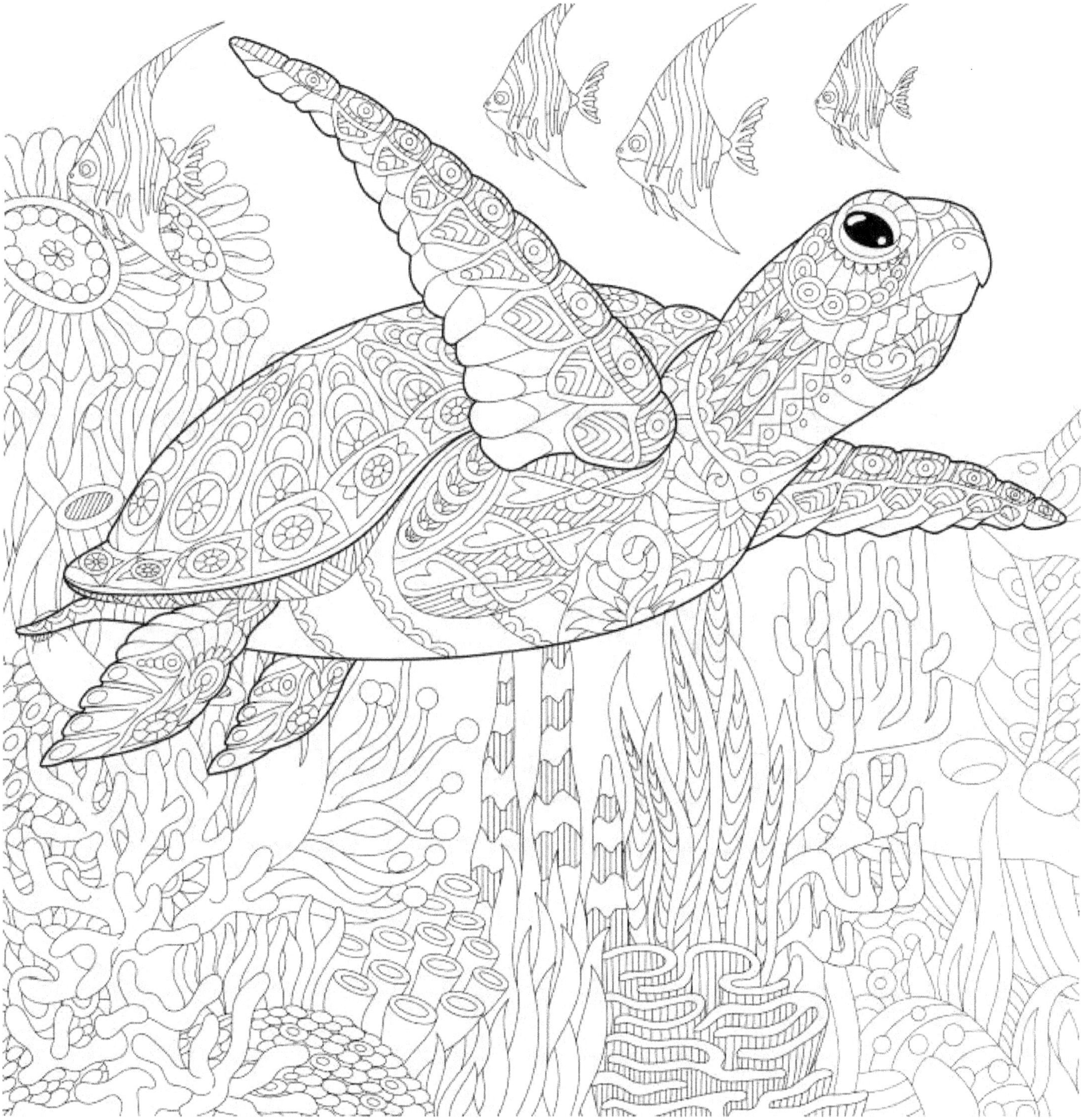

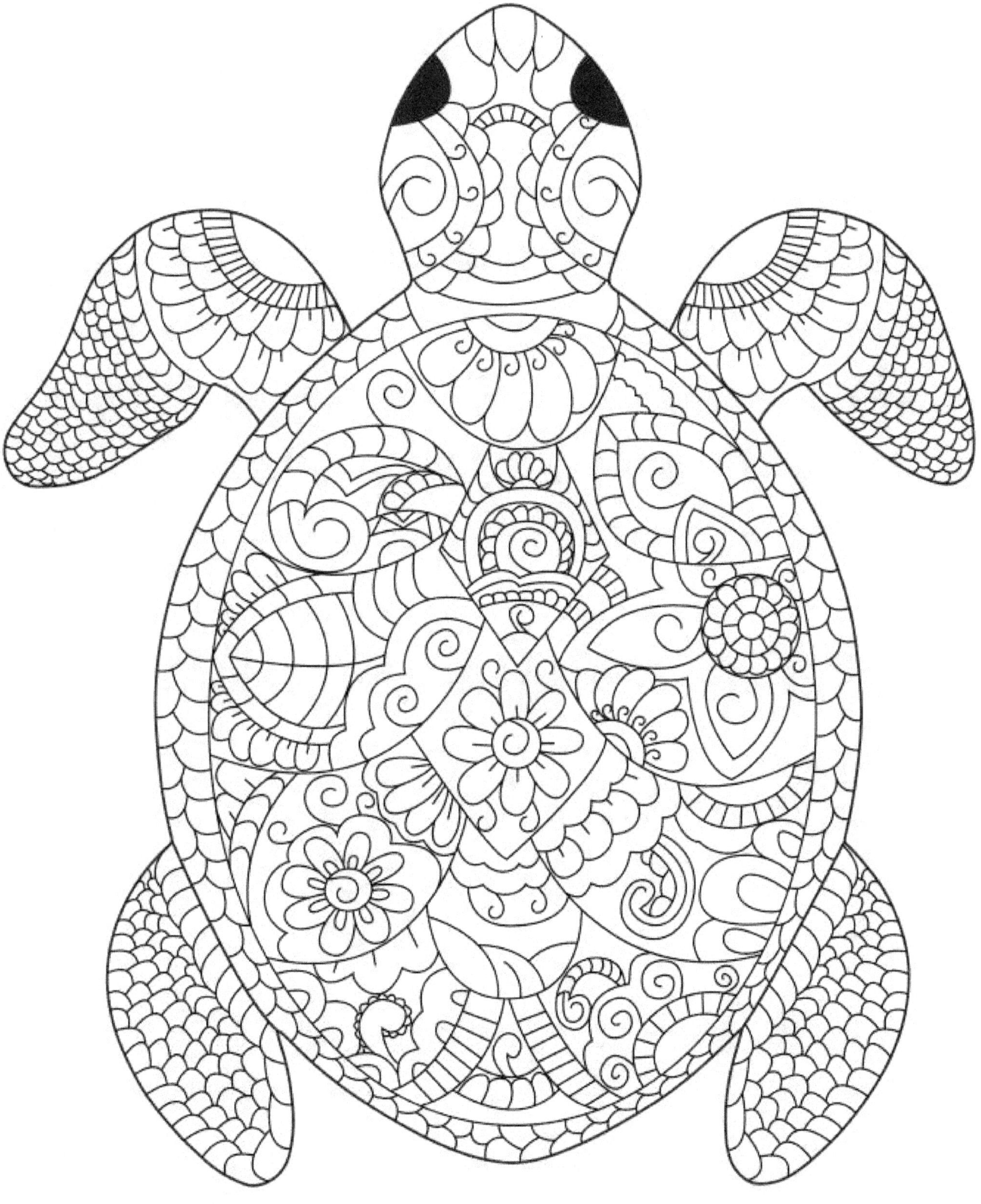

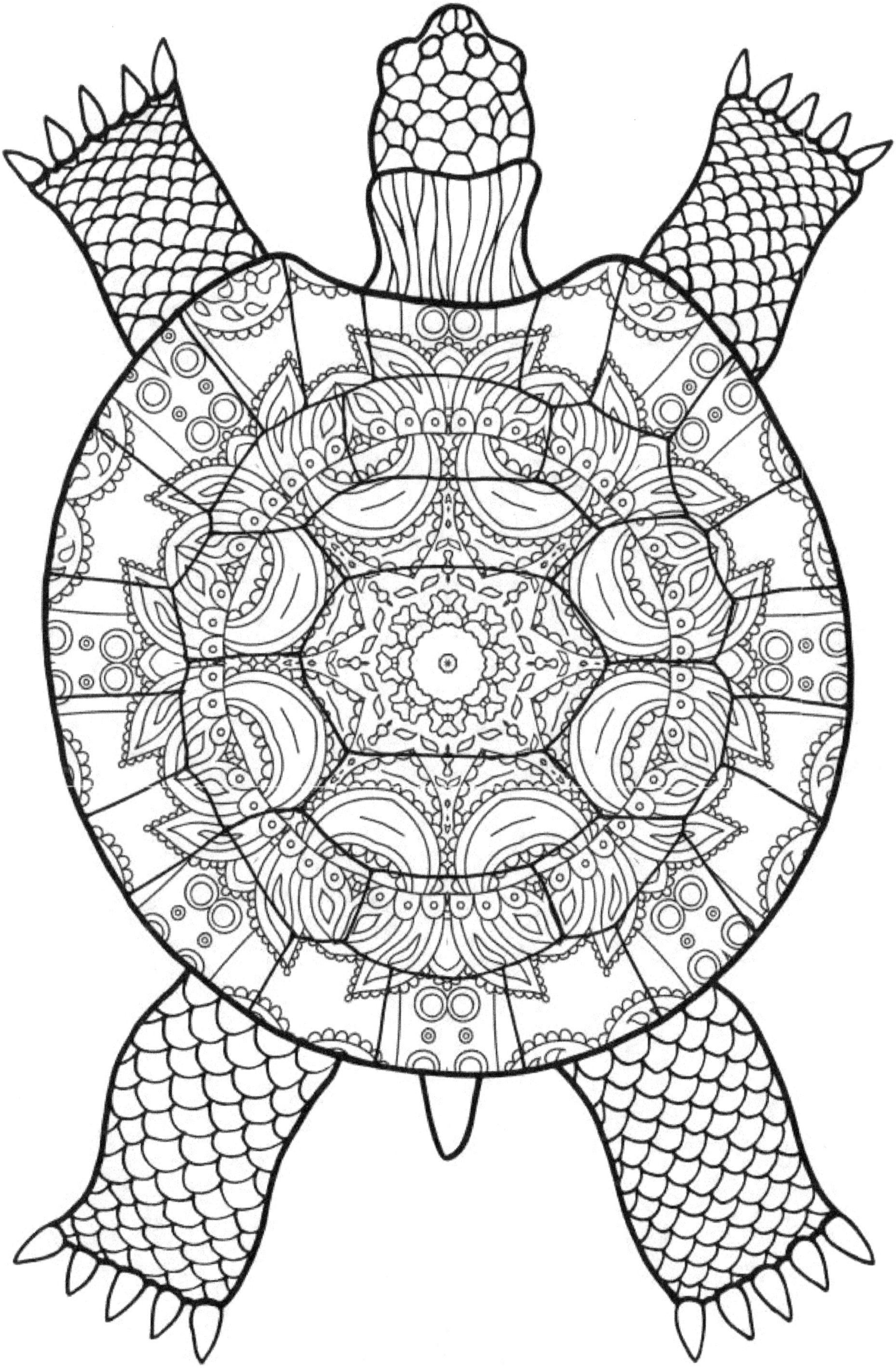

www.ingramcontent.com/pod-product-compliance
Lightning Source LLC
Chambersburg PA
CBHW081750170526
45167CB00009B/3989
* 9 7 8 1 5 4 4 0 4 3 3 3 3 *